a SAVOR THE SOUTH™ *cookbook*

Pecans

a SAVOR THE SOUTH™ *cookbook*

Pecans

KATHLEEN PURVIS

The University of North Carolina Press CHAPEL HILL

The paper in this book meets the guidelines for permanence and durability of
the Committee on Production Guidelines for Book Longevity of the Council on
Library Resources. The University of North Carolina Press has been a member
of the Green Press Initiative since 2003.

Library of Congress Cataloging-in-Publication Data
Purvis, Kathleen.
Pecans : a savor the South™ cookbook / Kathleen Purvis.
p. cm.
Includes index.
ISBN 978-0-8078-3579-1 (cloth: alk. paper) 1. Cooking (Pecans) 2. Cooking,
American—Southern style. I. Title.
TX814.P4P87 2012
641.6′452—dc23   2012010939

16 15 14 13 12   5 4 3 2 1

Contents

a SAVOR THE SOUTH™ *cookbook*

Pecans

Introduction

I keep my pecans in the freezer.

Yes, they last longer there, where the cold protects their rich oils and buttery texture. But the freezer doesn't just save my pecans from age.

It saves my pecans from me.

That's the idea, anyway. The truth is, I can't resist pecans. Never could. Put pecans in any dish, and I will crave it. Show me a recipe with pecans, and I have to try it. Put a bag of shelled pecans in my kitchen, and I will make excuses to dip into it every time it catches my eye.

Freezing them doesn't actually stop me from eating them. The little devils don't freeze hard, so even frozen, they're easy to eat. (Icy pecans mixed with a few dark chocolate morsels are even better, giving the chocolate a satisfying crunch. But perhaps I shouldn't put that idea in your head.) Still, hiding my pecans in the freezer at least slows me down a little.

My Georgia origins may be to blame for my inability to say no to a pecan. The state where I was born is still the nation's leader in growing pecans. Pecans and I both have deep roots in that red clay. Although I have lived all over the South, including eastern North Carolina and several parts of Florida, I was born in Georgia (Columbus) to a Georgia mother (Atlanta) and a Georgia father (Americus) with a hundred years of Georgians behind us.

With that background, we always had pecans in our house. My mother hardly made a cookie, candy, or pan of Sunday dressing without them. My grandmother's best recipes included them. It's hard to remember any occasion, from a picnic to a cocktail hour to a postfuneral spread, when pecans didn't turn up somewhere, mixed in the chicken salad, embedded in the cheese ball, sprinkled on the casserole, or just buttered, salted, and put out by the bowlful.

Family car trips in the summer always included a stop at a Stuckey's, where we'd beg for a pecan log. At the holidays, piles

1

of pecans went into my grandmother's special Nibble Mix, which she packed in empty coffee cans and mailed to family and friends scattered all over the South. Pecans in their woody shells filled the special bowl with the nutcracker that was always somewhere near my dad's TV chair in the winter.

On a shelf in my kitchen today, I have a black cast-iron nutcracker shaped like a dog, a replica of one that my mother remembers from her grandfather's desk. As a child, if she was good, she was allowed to put a pecan in the dog's jaws and pull down its tail to crack the nut.

For all my love of pecans, I sometimes hesitate to say the word. As a native of South Georgia, my father said "pee-can," a pronunciation that drew sniffs of disapproval from my mother, who would point out that a pee-can is something you keep under the bed. She grew up in more urbane Atlanta, where the nut was a "pah-cahn." No matter which way I said it, I could expect a rebuke from the other parent. By the time I was an adult, I had developed my own eccentric pronunciation, "pee-cahn."

When I began work on this book, I knew I was going to need a whopping amount of nuts. I went online and tracked down a good price from the Gilbert Pecan Company in Texas.

Georgia may be number 1 in pecan production, but Texas runs a close second. (New Mexico is creeping up there, too.)

After a phone chat with a very nice lady, I put in an order for thirty pounds of pecans. A few days later, a large cardboard box arrived on my doorstep. My husband and I hefted it onto the dining room table, slit open the tape, pulled back the flaps, and found ourselves gazing at the largest number of pecans we had ever seen at one time. They weren't bagged, just poured straight into the box, right up to the top.

As I grabbed my storage bags and went to work with a scale, I began to notice a heavenly scent. Even raw, that many pecans massed together have a distinct aroma. As I scooped, weighed, and bagged, I contemplated whether pecans actually smell like caramel, or whether so many things made with pecans include brown sugar that I associate their smell with caramel.

Whichever it is, if you ever get a chance to go face-down in thirty pounds of pecans, give a good sniff and let me know what you think.

What's a Pecan?

My favorite pecan story happened on my very first trip to New York City, the week before Thanksgiving in 1987, when I went up for a long weekend with my friend Kathy.

An early brutal cold snap hit the city, but we were young and city-struck enough that we didn't care. The fact that it was too cold to be outside just gave us an excuse to spend more time inside shopping, and we quickly headed for Macy's.

This was long before food-shopping wonderments like Eataly and the Chelsea Market. I hadn't yet seen the food halls at Harrods in London or trolled the cheese stalls of the Rue Mouffetard in Paris. That first experience in the Macy's basement was the closest thing to gourmet heaven I had ever seen.

While I wandered through aisles stocked with more kitchen tools than I could imagine using in a lifetime, Kathy stepped into a little alcove packed with holiday cooking ingredients, including a wooden barrel filled to the brim with shelled pecan halves.

Kathy picked out a few things and took her place in line behind a well-dressed woman of the Park Avenue variety.

When the woman's turn came, she slapped down a copy of the *New York Times* food section folded back to a Thanksgiving recipe.

"Miss," she said with sniffy hauteur. "Where are the pecan *meats*?"

The young clerk nodded at the large barrel of pecans just a few feet away.

Miss Park Avenue looked at them and shook her head.

"No," she said dismissively. "Those are just pecans. This recipe in the *Times* calls for pecan *meats*."

Kathy gathered her courage and leaned in to assure the woman, as a direct import from the South, that those were pecan meats, that "pecan meat" was just a fancy, *New York Times* way of referring to a shelled pecan.

The woman shook her off and insisted that was nonsense. The *Times* had not called for pecans. It had called for pecan *meats.*

Before Kathy could try again, the clerk looked the woman right in the eye and said calmly, "Oh, *pecan* meats. We're out of those. Try Zabar's."

The woman huffed off while the clerk smiled blandly at Kathy. Another dissatisfied customer was off her nerves and deftly transferred to someone else's.

Could we really be so confused about the native nut of America? Italy may have the pignoli and England can claim the walnut. But while America has an affection for the peanut (a nut in name only), the pecan is the true American nut, a native species that started right here.

Growing for the Future, Roots in the Past

Botanically, the pecan is a distant relative of the hickory. George Washington and Thomas Jefferson knew pecans. Although a few sources claim that Washington planted them first at Mount Vernon, most versions of the story are that Jefferson planted them, then sent some to Washington as a gift and urged him to plant them around 1775.

Neither man probably called them pecans, however. "Pecan" comes from an Algonquin word, "paccan" or "pakan," that means any nut hard enough to crack with a stone. Because fur trappers found pecans in southern Illinois and sent them east, early Americans called them Illinois nuts. The botanical name still reflects that: *Carya illinoinensis.* (I should probably acknowledge right here that botanically, a pecan isn't technically considered a nut. There are botanical debates on how to define many nuts, but in general, nuts such as almonds, walnuts, and pecans are defined as drupes, fruits with a central stone surrounded by a husk. But since that's splitting hairs finer than the arguments over whether a tomato is a fruit, we'll stick with the common classification of a pecan as a tree nut. After all, is how something grows more important than how it's used?)

Before America was completely settled, pecan trees were already growing along the Mississippi River, from southern Indiana to Texas, throughout the Southeast, and from the Southwest down into Mexico. It's impossible to say where they started because Native Americans carried them as they roamed. Wild pecans grew along waterways, so the nuts were easy to find and pack along as a portable source of protein.

Native Americans certainly made use of them. Spanish explorers found some tribes that would live solely on pecans for a couple of months a year. They not only ate the nuts but ground them to use as a flour or to mix with water to make a high-calcium drink.

As valuable as pecans were, it took a while for American settlers to figure out how to grow them commercially. Wild pecans don't grow true to the parent, so propagating a tree with reliable attributes was a tough nut to crack.

Abner Landrum of South Carolina figured out how to graft a pecan tree in 1822, but while his name was recorded, his method was lost. In 1846, at what is now known as Oak Alley Plantation in Louisiana, a horticulturist named A. E. Colomb was invited to visit while he worked on a grafting project. Colomb was assisted by an Oak Alley slave named Antoine, who was known as a gifted gardener. Colomb died in 1848, but Antoine successfully completed the project, creating a grafted tree with large, thin-shelled nuts that are believed to be the first papershell pecans.

Despite the success of Antoine's trees, they were cut down after the Civil War. But offshoots of the original tree had been planted in other locations, so it wasn't lost. A descendant of Antoine's tree was entered in the Centennial Exhibition in Philadelphia in 1876, where it won a prize and was renamed the Centennial. The tree was so successful, it became the basis for commercial pecan production. Today, there are hundreds of pecan varieties, from the Elliott to the Stuart to the Cape Fear.

A pecan tree is a mighty endeavor. Growing up to 130 feet tall with a naturally graceful canopy spreading from a single trunk, pecans typically live and can bear nuts for a hundred years or more. The oldest pecan tree on record is 300 years old.

Lenny Wells, a pecan horticulturist with the University of Georgia, is based in Tifton, the center of American pecan production. He spends his days surrounded by pecan trees.

When you work with pecan trees, he says, you're working for the future. "Rather than having a row crop, like cotton or soybeans, that you plant every year, a tree is something you plant that's going to be there longer than you're going to be there."

Pecan trees bear alternately, with a heavy year followed by a light year. The tree produces hormones based on its crop load, so when it has a heavy crop, hormones tell the tree to produce fewer nuts the next year. The variation in output becomes more extreme as the tree gets older, so some growers replace trees once they reach sixty to eighty years old. The older trees also get so large that they become difficult to spray and harvest.

When you drive through South Georgia, it's easy to spot a pecan grove. The huge trees are planted in long rows, often covering acres and marching right up to the porches of gracious old homes. A pecan grove really is something you plant and nurture with an eye toward future generations.

When my husband and I drive through South Georgia in early winter on the way to spend Thanksgiving with family in Tallahassee, Florida, I love to watch for large balls of vines way up at the tops of the trees. That's mistletoe, and it's a southern tradition to go out into pecan groves with shotguns in the winter, fire up into the trees, and knock down sprigs for Christmas decorations.

Unfortunately, as pretty as mistletoe is, it's a pest. Mistletoe is a parasite, sucking nutrients and water from the tree and limiting the crop. The only way to eradicate it is by pruning. But since it's spread by birds, the clusters grow high in the trees and are hard to reach, so they generally stay where they are.

If pecans grow in such a wide area, why have Georgia and Texas dominated the American market? There are a couple of stories about that.

Texas's pecan industry has a turn-of-the-century governor to thank, James S. Hogg, father of the famous heiress Ima Hogg. Wild pecan trees once grew all over Texas, but they were cut severely to make room for cotton fields. Hogg loved the trees, though. Just before he died in 1906, he said he wanted a pecan tree and a walnut tree planted at his grave in place of a tombstone, and he wanted the nuts given to people to plant so Texas would become "a land of trees." It captured the Texas imagination so much that in 1916, the pecan was named the Texas state tree. (It's the state tree of Alabama, too.)

Georgia, though, surpassed Texas in marketing and eventually in pecan growing. As a rural state, Georgia wanted to attract settlement. From about 1900 through the Depression, pecans became part of a popular real-estate scheme. Developers would buy tracts of land, plant pecan trees, and then advertise the land in five-acre plots as pecan "plantations" that would pay for themselves. Of course, the ads often made grand claims for how much the trees could be expected to produce and how little work would be involved in caring for them.

"They'd tell you you'd be able to harvest some ridiculous amount of pecans and you'd never have to worry about retirement or your children's education," says Lenny Wells. "They didn't have the irrigation and the land practices we have now, and it would take the trees longer to begin producing."

Even though the claims didn't live up to their hype, Georgia ended up being planted with thousands and thousands of acres of pecan trees. Luckily, there were legitimate growers, too, and pecans did so well in Georgia that they shaped the agriculture of the state.

Those orderly rows of trees you see in a pecan grove came from a clever farming practice. It takes ten to twelve years for a pecan tree to begin bearing well. Meanwhile, a peach tree will bear more quickly, within a couple of years, but it will only last about fifteen years.

So, many pecan groves actually started as peach orchards. You'd alternate a row of pecans with a row of peaches, and just about the time the peach tree reached the end of its productivity, the pecan tree was revving up. Pull out the peach, and you had room for the pecan tree to keep growing for decades, eventually developing a trunk that was more than six feet around.

Georgia may call itself the Peach State, but it's really nuts for pecans.

Good for You, Pecan Eater

Those Native Americans who packed pecans into their diets knew what they were doing. All nuts are nutritional powerhouses relative to their size, but current research shows that pecans have particularly helpful attributes.

While all nuts are high in fat, most of it—90 percent in the case of pecans—is heart-healthy unsaturated fat. In addition, nuts are high in protein and have no cholesterol or sodium (at least, not until we roast them and toss them with salt).

Along with that, pecans deliver a packet of nutrients, including vitamin A, which is good for our teeth, eyes, and bones; a form of vitamin E; calcium; magnesium; potassium; and zinc, among a long list of minerals. Plus, nuts include fiber, which helps us feel full longer.

What nutritionists really are excited about, however, are two other recent findings. First, there is evidence that pecans contain more antioxidants than any other tree nut, according to the USDA Antioxidant Nutrient Database. While some studies have shown that walnuts rate higher, it depends on how the laboratory analysis is done. Most sources give the USDA's analysis more weight, putting pecans in the lead. Antioxidants are believed to help us resist disease by protecting the body against cell damage.

Second, a study at Loma Linda University, reported in the *Journal of Nutrition* in January 2011, found evidence that consumption of pecans decreases LDL, the so-called bad cholesterol that leads to heart disease.

Of course, there is a downside to all this good news. Nuts usually don't come into our diets without company, mainly salt, sugar, and butter. Just because a small serving of pecans a day—eighteen to twenty halves—is a good idea, that doesn't mean a slice of pecan pie is something you should eat every day. I'll leave that decision up to you and your scale.

Nature gives nuts a lot of protection. To get to the meat (yes, the part you eat is sometimes called a nutmeat), you have to get through the shell.

I never crack a pecan without thinking of a nice lady named Lee.

My husband is a native of Tallahassee, a lovely town in the Florida Panhandle where the streets are shaded by arching tunnels of live oaks and the yards are graced with pecan trees. Walking to classes at Florida State University in the fall, you had to watch your step: There were so many pecans hidden under the fallen oak leaves that it was like walking on ball bearings.

My husband and I met at the *Tallahassee Democrat*, where I was a young reporter and Wayne was a pasteup artist who helped build the paper. Since so many artists went to FSU, the pasteup crew was mostly young, artistic, and male.

Lee was a typesetter, an older woman with a heavy Long Island accent. As they say in the South, she was "not from around here," but she had a real affection for the young guys on pasteup.

One afternoon, they came to work and found two gorgeous pecan pies. Lee had decided to try her hand at some real southern cooking.

You don't have to tell a bunch of young men to grab forks and dig in. They happily cut big slabs of pie and started to eat. My husband still remembers the horror: a sweet bite of pie followed by stabbing pain and the awful, astringent taste of that pithy dark stuff that grows around pecans inside their shells.

No one wanted to hurt Lee's feelings, so they asked carefully: "Um, Lee—where'd you get these pecans?"

Oh, she had bought a whole bag of them in the shell. She wanted to really make her pies from scratch. But they were so much trouble, she mused. All that cracking and picking out the bits of shell. She figured no one really goes to all that trouble. So she finally gave up and just threw it all in, shells, pith, and all.

No, no, no, people. Do not let this happen to you. Yes, you have to shell pecans and pick away all that pithy brown material, especially the bits that cling to the nut's natural ridges. There is a reason shelled pecans cost so much more than pecans in the shell. It is a fair amount of work to separate the nut from the shell.

The wild pecans that the Native Americans knew had harder shells that really did have to be cracked with stones. But starting with Antoine in Louisiana, commercial growers cultivated trees with nuts that have thinner shells, called papershell pecans. When pecans are brought to market, the price is set by the size of the kernel, or nutmeat, relative to the shell. The thinner the shell, the larger the nut can grow inside it. Papershell varieties have shells so thin you can crack them by holding two in your hand and squeezing.

There's a trade-off, though. The shell protects the nut, after all. If it gets too thin, it can leave the nut vulnerable to damage from storms or pests. So growers aim for a sweet spot between a shell that is thick enough to protect the nut and one that isn't too hard to crack.

Shelling pecans doesn't have to be an odious task. Like a lot of other cooking chores—shelling peas, grating cheese, whisking vinaigrettes—there's a Zen aspect to it. On a sunny fall afternoon, sitting on the patio with newspaper spread out to catch the shells and a bowl in my lap to catch the pecans is a pleasant way to spend an hour.

How to shell the pecans? There are dozens of styles of nutcrackers out there, from that primitive black cast-iron dog to much fancier spring-loaded contraptions. When I was a child, our house nutcracker was shaped like a hollow metal pecan with a big screw. You placed the pecan inside with the top fitted into a notch at the bottom of the screw and spun the screw down to snap open the shell. You had to wrap your hand around the nutcracker to keep the nut from jumping out. If you weren't careful, your palm would get pinched between the nut and the screw. Just thinking about it still makes my hand hurt a little.

Forget that. Let me introduce you to my little friend, the Reed's Rocket.

The Rocket is a brilliantly simple contraption, with a sliding metal barrel attached to a small wooden base and a handle that screws into place. You can adjust the slide mechanism to handle anything from a hazelnut to a Brazil nut. With enough elbow grease, it can even crack the notoriously hard black walnut. It's a wonder at accommodating the elongated shape of a pecan. Once you get the opening adjusted correctly, you can work at a steady pace, getting the leverage just right to crack open the shell without crushing the nut inside. It's exactly what you need to produce a bowl that's mostly nut halves with the minimum number of broken pieces.

Look for the Reed's Rocket, in its retro-style box, at hardware stores or find it online. Then just take a seat outside, spread out a sheet of newspaper, and go to town. You can even recycle the broken shells on your flower beds. That's what my grandmother did.

Once you have your pecans shelled, make sure you store them in the freezer. With their rich oils, they will get rancid at room temperature very quickly, but they'll keep for months in an airtight bag in the freezer. If you can hide them well enough, that is.

Tips for Pecan Cooks

✳ Save time measuring: If a recipe calls for 1 cup chopped pecans, measure out 1 cup whole, shelled nuts and chop them. You'll end up having the same amount as you would if you chopped the nuts and then measured them.

✳ Pecans burn easily. Instead of toasting them in the oven where you can't see them as easily, toast them in a dry skillet on the stove over medium heat. It's easier to stir them frequently, you can stay close by to watch for burning, and you'll be able to smell when they're getting fragrant—or moving from fragrant to scorched.

✳ Pecans keep best—and cost less—if you buy them in the shell. Once they're shelled, store them in heavy-duty resealable bags in the freezer. They'll keep fine for up to a year.

Appetizers and Party Foods

So many party foods include pecans that just putting them out seems to be an inspiration for good times. Roasted pecans are such an entertaining essential that I couldn't stop with just one recipe. Instead, I created four, including one based on the classic cocktail, the Old-Fashioned, which features a pecan-infused bourbon. I then branched out into spreads, dips, and salty/crunchy snacks.

When you're choosing pecan recipes, remember that pecans play particularly well with cheeses of any kind, but especially sharp cheddar and blue cheese; Dijon mustard; garlic; Worcestershire sauce; butter; honey; oranges; and strawberries.

Basic Buttered, Salted Pecans

Consider these the little black dress of appetizers. There just isn't anything better to have with cocktails, particularly bourbon. I tried every method, from oven roasting to sautéing in butter, and finally settled on this very simple version as the best. Roasting often makes them taste burned, and browning the butter while sautéing can overwhelm the taste of the pecans.

MAKES 3 CUPS

---

3 cups pecan halves
1 tablespoon unsalted butter
1 teaspoon kosher salt

Spread the pecans in a single layer in a large skillet. Place over medium heat. Cook, stirring frequently and watching carefully for scorching, for about 8–10 minutes. The pecans should be very fragrant and just starting to darken but should not have any burned spots. If you see any burned pecans, remove the skillet from the heat immediately.

Pour the hot pecans in a heatproof bowl. Add the butter and stir until it is melted and the pecans are lightly coated. Sprinkle with the salt, stirring to coat. Cool and store in an airtight container.

Smoky Garlic-Mustard Pecans

Liquid smoke is an odd ingredient. Although some people think it's a chemical concoction, it's actually just water infused with smoke. The taste can be very strong, though, so be careful not to use too much. If you don't like it or don't have it, skip it; the pecans won't taste smoky, but they'll still taste good.

MAKES 2 CUPS

4 tablespoons melted unsalted butter
1 teaspoon dry mustard
2 teaspoons garlic powder
1 teaspoon Lawry's Seasoned Salt
1 teaspoon sugar
1 tablespoon Dijon mustard
1½ teaspoons Worcestershire sauce
¼ teaspoon liquid smoke
2 cups pecan halves
1 teaspoon sea salt

Preheat the oven to 250°.

Whisk together the melted butter, dry mustard, garlic powder, seasoned salt, sugar, Dijon mustard, Worcestershire sauce, and liquid smoke in a mixing bowl. Add the pecans and stir until they are well coated.

Spread the pecans in a single layer on a rimmed baking sheet. Bake for 20–30 minutes, stirring every 5–10 minutes. Remove from the oven and immediately sprinkle with the sea salt. Cool and store in an airtight container for up to 3 days.

Sweet Heat Sriracha Pecans

I know people who claim to be addicted to the iconic Thai hot sauce with the rooster on the label. To me, it has great flavor, but it calls out for a second dimension. Like sweet. Hmm . . .

MAKES 2 CUPS

4 tablespoons honey
2 tablespoons Sriracha chili sauce
2 cups pecan halves
3 tablespoons sugar
2 teaspoons kosher salt

Preheat the oven to 325°. Spread out a sheet of aluminum foil.

Combine the honey and Sriracha in a small saucepan and warm over medium-low heat until liquefied and well mixed.

Remove from the heat and add the pecans. Stir well with a wooden spoon or rubber spatula until the pecans are lightly coated and the honey mixture is used up.

Spread the pecans on a rimmed baking sheet in a single layer. Bake for 15 minutes.

While the pecans are baking, combine the sugar and salt in a heatproof bowl. When the pecans are done, scrape them into the bowl with the sugar/salt mixture. Stir until the pecans are completely coated and the sugar mixture is used up. Spread on the foil and let cool. Store in an airtight container for up to 5 days.

Bourbon-Orange Pecans

My husband, the beloved Mr. Wayne, is a master of classic cock-tails. Since one of his house specialties is the Old-Fashioned, I wanted a nibble that would match the flavors of orange, bourbon, and bitters.

MAKES 3 CUPS

½ cup sugar
½ teaspoon salt
1 tablespoon grated orange zest
½ teaspoon cayenne pepper
2 large egg whites
3 tablespoons bourbon
3 cups pecan halves

Preheat the oven to 300°.

Mix the sugar, salt, orange zest, and cayenne pepper in a small bowl.

Beat the egg whites with an electric mixer until soft peaks form (they should curl over when the beaters are lifted). Beat in the bourbon.

Fold in the pecans with a rubber spatula until well coated. Add the sugar mixture and fold to coat well.

Spread the pecans on a rimmed baking sheet. Bake for 30 minutes, stirring every 10 minutes. The coating will foam up but will stir down, and the pecans will become crisp and will separate as they bake. Remove from the oven. Cool and break apart the individual nuts. Store in an airtight container for up to 1 week.

Pecan-Orange Bourbon

Bourbon and pecans go together so well that it was no surprise when trendy mixologists started infusing bourbon with pecans a couple of years ago. I think the hint of orange makes the flavor perfect. You can use the result in any bourbon cocktail, but the spicy flavor is perfect in an Old-Fashioned (page 19).

MAKES ABOUT 1 PINT

1 cup pecan halves
3–4 long strips of orange zest
2 cups bourbon

Preheat the oven to 300°.

Cover the pecans with water and let stand for 30 minutes. Drain. Spread the pecans on a rimmed baking sheet and bake for 20 minutes.

Place the warm pecans in a jar with a tight-fitting lid and add the orange zest and bourbon. Cover and let stand at room temperature for 4–5 days, shaking daily.

Strain the bourbon into a storage container, discarding the pecans and orange zest. Use the bourbon in a cocktail or straight up over ice.

NOTE ✻ It would be nice to be able to roast and eat the bourbon-soaked pecans, but I'll save you the trouble. It is important to soak and then roast the pecans before adding them to the bourbon to reduce some of the natural fat. This keeps the bourbon from being too heavy, but it also renders the pecans unsuitable for further use. They take on a waxy consistency, which makes them unpleasant to eat. Just discard them and make a separate batch for eating. Bourbon-Orange Pecans (page 17) are perfect.

Old-Fashioned

If you don't make this with the pecan-infused bourbon, try it with a batch of Bourbon-Orange Pecans (page 17).

MAKES 1 SERVING

1 teaspoon simple syrup or granulated sugar
3 dashes bitters (preferably Fee Brothers Old Fashion Bitters)
¼ of an orange slice
1 maraschino cherry
2 ounces Pecan-Orange Bourbon (page 18)
Sparkling water or club soda

To prepare the simple syrup, combine 1 cup sugar and 1 cup water in a small saucepan over medium heat. Heat, stirring, until the sugar is completely dissolved. Remove from the heat, cool, and refrigerate until needed.

Place the simple syrup or sugar, bitters, orange, and cherry in a double rocks glass. Press lightly with a muddler or spoon. Fill the glass halfway with ice and add the bourbon. Stir briefly and top with sparkling water or club soda. Stir once very gently.

Nibble Mix

Some grandmothers teach you polite skills like knitting. My grandmother, Caroline Simmons of Atlanta, Georgia, was a painter and florist who taught me how to make a martini and perfected Nibble Mix, the quintessential cocktail nosh. Every Christmas, she mailed us a coffee can full of it. Yes, the recipe is so common today that you can buy prepackaged versions, but those pale in comparison to my grandmother's. The stained recipe card my mother copied out for me specifies the amount of pecans to be "as many as you can afford." She was a child of the Depression and never changed.

MAKES ABOUT 6 QUARTS

½ cup plus 1 tablespoon vegetable oil
1 clove garlic, cut in half
Cheerios
Rice Chex
Wheat Chex
Cheddar-flavored fish-shaped crackers
Skinny pretzel sticks
2–3 cups pecan halves
Lawry's Seasoned Salt
Garlic powder
1⅓ sticks melted unsalted butter
About ¼ cup Worcestershire sauce

Preheat the oven to 275°.

Put 1 tablespoon oil in the biggest roasting pan you have. Rub the oil all over the pan using the cut sides of the garlic halves, then discard the garlic.

Pour the cereal into the pan: about a half of a box of Cheerios, a half of a box of Rice Chex, a third of a box of Wheat Chex, a whole bag of cheddar fish-shaped crackers, several large handfuls of pretzel sticks, and the pecans.

Pour ½ cup vegetable oil over it all and mix well. Sprinkle generously with seasoned salt and garlic powder and stir.

Bake for 15 minutes. Remove from the oven and stir well. (I use a metal spatula to get all the way down to the bottom of the pan and turn everything well.) Return to the oven for 15 minutes.

Combine the melted butter with the Worcestershire sauce. (The only way to determine the right amount of Worcestershire sauce is to smell it: It should be pungent enough to feel it in the back of your throat.)

Remove the pan from the oven. Drizzle the flavored butter evenly over the mix and stir. Return to the oven for 15 minutes. Stir again and bake 15 minutes longer, 1 hour in all. Cool and store in large metal or airtight plastic containers. Give away to close friends and family. Make at least one more batch to use up the rest of the cereal. When the Nibble Mix is gone, it's time to take down the tree and declare that Christmas is over.

Blue Cheese Pecan Spread

Pecans play well with so many cheeses, but something special happens when you put them together with blue cheese. The buttery nuts highlight the sharpness of the cheese.

MAKES 1 ½ CUPS

1 cup pecans

1 (8-ounce) package cream cheese, at room temperature

½ cup crumbled blue cheese

¼ cup snipped chives, divided

¼ teaspoon coarsely ground black pepper

Place the pecans in a dry skillet over medium heat. Stir often until fragrant and just toasted. Remove from the skillet and chop coarsely.

Place the cream cheese and blue cheese in a food processor. Pulse until creamy and combined. Set aside 1 tablespoon chives and add the rest to the food processor with the pepper. Pulse to combine. Add the pecans and pulse until just combined. (Don't overprocess; you want the pecans in chunks.)

Scrape into a small serving bowl or crock. Sprinkle the top with the remaining chives. Refrigerate until ready to serve. Serve with crackers.

Pecan Pimento Cheese

When it comes to pimento cheese, I'm usually of the "less is more" camp. But the version made by my friend Rebecca Fant, with cream cheese and pecans, proves that even perfection can be improved upon. She credits it to her mother-in-law, Sara Lynn Alday McCray.

MAKES ABOUT 4 CUPS

1 pound sharp cheddar cheese, shredded
1 (8-ounce) package cream cheese, at room temperature
½ cup mayonnaise, or to taste
1–1½ teaspoons Tabasco
1 (7-ounce) jar diced pimentos, undrained
1 cup chopped pecans

Combine the cheddar and cream cheese in a food processor, pulsing to mix. Mix in the mayonnaise and Tabasco. Scrape into a mixing bowl and stir in the pimentos and their juice and the pecans. Refrigerate until ready to serve. Serve with crackers.

Cheddar-Pecan Wafers

My good friend Brenda Pinnell is the queen of great holiday-party food. Luckily, she's just as generous with her recipes. This makes enough dough that you can tuck a bunch in the freezer and pull it out whenever you need a little something to take to a party.

MAKES ABOUT 200 CRACKERS

1 cup pecan halves
2 sticks plus 1 tablespoon unsalted butter
Kosher salt
1 pound extra-sharp cheddar cheese, shredded
2 cups all-purpose flour
1 teaspoon cayenne

Spread the pecans in a single layer in a dry skillet over medium heat and toast, stirring often and watching closely, until lightly browned and fragrant. Pour the pecans into a heatproof bowl and immediately add 1 tablespoon butter and salt to taste. Stir until the butter is melted and the pecans are coated. Cool the pecans completely, then finely chop them.

Place the cheese in a large mixing bowl. Cut 2 sticks butter into 16 pieces and scatter over the top of the cheese. Let stand for 10 minutes or so to soften the butter. Add the nuts, flour, and cayenne and beat with an electric mixer until it forms a dough.

Tear off 8 squares of wax paper. Divide the dough into 8 portions. Shape each portion into a 1½-inch-diameter log, rolling to smooth the sides, then wrap each log in wax paper. Refrigerate for at least 8 hours or up to 1 week (or freeze for up to 2 months).

Preheat the oven to 350°. Line a baking sheet with parchment paper.

Working with 1 log at a time, use a sharp knife to cut ⅛-inch-thick slices and arrange them ½ inch apart on the parchment paper. (If the logs are frozen, they don't need to thaw completely. Just let them sit at room temperature until you can slice them.)

Bake for 10–12 minutes, until the wafers are just golden; some will be bubbly around the edges. Remove from the oven and let stand for about 2 minutes. Use a metal spatula to remove them from the sheet and place them on a wire rack. While they're still warm, turn them over and sprinkle them with a little salt (it sticks better to the crevices on the underside). Store in an airtight container for up to 4 days.

Tallahassee Cheese Ring

When my husband's parents celebrated their sixtieth anniversary, the buzz at the buffet was about a delicious cheese spread topped with strawberry jam. I charged into the kitchen and bugged the caterer, who confessed it was an old recipe associated with First Lady Rosalynn Carter. The combination of onion, cheddar, and strawberry was almost perfect. Almost: How could a great Georgia recipe be missing pecans?

MAKES 10–12 SERVINGS

8 ounces sharp cheddar, finely shredded
8 ounces medium cheddar, finely shredded
4 green onions, white and some of the green, chopped
½ teaspoon cayenne pepper
4–6 tablespoons mayonnaise
½ cup toasted, chopped pecans
About ½ cup strawberry jam

Place the cheeses, green onions, and cayenne and 4–5 tablespoons mayonnaise in a food processor. Process until smooth, adding another tablespoon of mayonnaise if needed.

Place the cheese on a serving plate and shape into a ring with a well pressed into the center. Press the pecans into the outer edge of the ring. Spoon the strawberry jam into the indentation in the center. Refrigerate until ready to serve. Serve with crackers.

French Bread Baked Brie

I have taken this to many holiday parties, assembled and ready to bake. Put it out on the table warm from the oven, and all you have to do at the end of the night is gather the empty dish. You can divide the recipe if you prefer.

MAKES ABOUT 16 SERVINGS

Nonstick cooking spray
2 (11-ounce) spiral cans refrigerated French bread dough
2 cold (8–10 ounce) Brie rounds
4 tablespoons raspberry jam
½ cup chopped pecans
2 tablespoons light brown sugar

Preheat the oven to 350°. Spray two 1 ½-quart gratin dishes, two tart pans, or a large baking sheet with nonstick cooking spray. Place each Brie in a gratin dish, in a tart pan, or on the baking sheet with plenty of space in between.

Open the cans of French bread dough. Wrap the dough once around each Brie, twisting as you go. Press the ends together. With kitchen scissors or a sharp knife, make cuts into the dough at regular intervals, about 2 inches apart.

Spread the jam on top of the cheese, then sprinkle each with the pecans and brown sugar.

Bake for 30 minutes, then cool for 15 minutes. (These can stand for up to 1 hour after baking if needed. Wrap them tightly to transport them.) Cut into wedges to serve.

Praline Brie

As a church food director, my friend Nancy McGinnis knows just what to make for weddings and special occasions. Her version of baked Brie, with orange marmalade, is a combination that people can't resist.

MAKES 6–10 SERVINGS, DEPENDING
ON THE SIZE OF THE CHEESE

1 (7–13 ounce) Brie round
½ cup orange marmalade
2 tablespoons light brown sugar
⅓ cup toasted, chopped pecans

Preheat the oven to 350°.

Place the Brie in a shallow baking dish or pie plate. Stir together the marmalade and brown sugar. Spoon it over the top of the Brie, letting some of it pool around the base. Sprinkle with the pecans, and bake for 15 minutes. Serve warm with apple or baguette slices or crackers.

Main Dishes

Pecans are natural additions to entrées, contributing meatiness and crunchiness as well as a touch of elegance. Chicken, pork, and fish dishes all work beautifully with nuts. Honey, Dijon mustard, and chicken are so perfect with pecans that I couldn't resist creating several versions. Pecan Pesto is always a surprise, even better than the traditional version. But my favorite pecan entrée is Pecan-Crusted Grouper with a luxurious wine and butter sauce.

Which wine to drink with pecans? Instead of the bitterness of walnuts, pecans have a natural creaminess that makes them an interesting match. My friend Catherine Rabb is a chef and a beverage instructor at Johnson & Wales University's Charlotte campus. She's also working on her certification as a master of wine. She's paired pecan pie with Madeira and very sweet sherry with butter pecan ice cream. But she still remembers the first time she had a classic trout fillet sautéed in brown butter with toasted pecans. "I wasn't even old enough to drink, but a more experienced co-worker had me try the fish with a buttery, nutty Cakebread Chardonnay from California. I mark that as one of the first times I realized that you could take a food and a wine that were fantastic alone and make them even better together."

Fruity, Nutty Chicken Salad

This isn't a chicken salad for a sandwich. It's more substantial, with lots of textures and crunch. Serve it on a bed of lettuce with crackers as a nice lunch or a light supper.

MAKES 4–6 SERVINGS

2 large eggs

1½ cups coarsely chopped pecans

4–6 cups cooked, chopped chicken (see Note below)

2 stalks celery, diced

2 cups halved red seedless grapes

½ cup mayonnaise, or to taste

½ teaspoon salt

1 teaspoon dried thyme

½ teaspoon dry mustard

½ teaspoon curry powder

Place the eggs in a small saucepan and cover with water. Bring to a boil. Cover the pan and remove from the heat. Let stand for 18 minutes. Rinse the eggs to cool, then peel and dice. Place in a large serving bowl.

While the eggs are cooking, place the pecans in a dry skillet over medium-low to medium heat. Stir frequently until toasted and fragrant. Cool, then add to serving bowl.

Add the chicken, celery, and grapes. Stir to combine. Add the mayonnaise, salt, thyme, dry mustard, and curry powder. Mix well. Taste and adjust seasonings and mayonnaise.

NOTE ❋ If you don't have cooked chicken on hand, poach skinless, boneless chicken breasts: Place 2 cups water, 1 cube chicken bouillon, and 1 cup dry vermouth (or 2 cups chicken stock) in a skillet. Bring to a simmer and stir until the bouillon is dissolved. Add 4 chicken breasts. Cover the skillet and cook gently for 15–20 minutes, until the chicken is cooked through. Remove from the heat and let stand until the chicken is cool enough to handle. Discard the poaching liquid or save it as the base for a soup.

Buttermilk-Pecan Chicken

This is easy enough for a satisfying weeknight dinner. The buttermilk and the pecan coating keep the skinless chicken breasts from getting dried out and give them more texture.

MAKES 4–6 SERVINGS

4 tablespoons unsalted butter
½ cup pecan meal or finely ground pecans (see Note below)
½ cup all-purpose flour
1 teaspoon smoked paprika
½ teaspoon salt
¼ teaspoon freshly ground black pepper
1 large egg
1 cup buttermilk
4–6 skinless, boneless chicken breasts
½ cup coarsely chopped pecans

Preheat the oven to 350°. Place the butter in a 13 × 9-inch baking dish and put the dish in the oven until the butter is melted, about 5 minutes.

Place the pecan meal and flour in a shallow dish, such as a pie plate. Add the paprika, salt, and pepper and whisk to combine.

Beat the egg lightly in another shallow dish. Whisk in the buttermilk. Dip the chicken breasts in the buttermilk mixture, turning to coat. Let stand for a minute or two.

Working with one breast at a time, remove the chicken pieces from the buttermilk mixture and let the excess drip off. Place in the pecan meal mixture, turning to coat thoroughly. Place in the baking dish with the melted butter and turn over to coat.

Repeat with the remaining chicken breasts. Sprinkle with the chopped pecans.

Bake for 30 minutes.

NOTE ❁ For the ground pecans, either use pecan meal, which is sold at some stores, or chop the pecans finely with a handheld or electric chopper or pulse in a food processor.

Shrimp and Farfalle with Pecan Pesto

Yes, you can make pesto with pecans. They're a bit cheaper than pine nuts, and the pesto has a meatier flavor. Even if you don't make this summer supper, a batch of Pecan Pesto in the freezer comes in handy all year.

MAKES 4 SERVINGS

FOR THE PECAN PESTO

2 cups basil leaves

$1/4$ cup pecan halves

2 cloves garlic

$1/2$ cup olive oil

$1/2$ cup grated Pecorino Romano cheese

Salt and freshly ground black pepper

FOR THE PASTA

8 ounces farfalle (bow-tie pasta)

1 pound shrimp, peeled and deveined, tails on if you prefer

1 cup frozen peas

$1/4$ cup roasted red pepper, cut in strips

$1/2$ cup coarsely chopped pecans

To make the pesto, place the basil, pecans, and garlic in a food processor and pulse to chop. With the motor running, slowly drizzle in the oil. Scrape the mixture into a small bowl and stir in the cheese. Season to taste with salt and pepper. The pesto can be made ahead. Drizzle a little oil over the top, cover well with plastic wrap, and refrigerate for up to 48 hours or freeze until needed.

Bring a large pot of salted water to a boil. Add the pasta and cook according to the label directions, generally about 11 minutes. Three minutes before the pasta is done, add the shrimp. After 2 minutes, add the peas. Reserve ½ cup cooking water, then drain the pasta, shrimp, and peas.

Return to the warm cooking pot and add the Pecan Pesto. Stir to coat well. Add a splash or two of the pasta-cooking water to form a sauce. Stir in the red pepper and remaining pecans and toss to combine everything.

Honey-Pecan Chicken

Classic flavors come together in a simple dish that's just right for a weeknight. It's perfect paired with wild rice.

1 teaspoon unsalted butter
1/3 cup honey
1/3 cup Dijon mustard
1/4 teaspoon salt
1/4 teaspoon freshly ground black pepper
4 skinless, boneless chicken breasts
1/3 cup coarsely chopped pecans

Preheat the oven to 350°. Butter an 8- or 9-inch square baking dish.

Whisk together the honey, mustard, salt, and pepper. Place the chicken breasts, top-side down, in the baking dish. Drizzle about half the mustard mixture over them, spreading it with a kitchen brush or the back of a spoon to coat the breasts. Turn the breasts over and coat the other side with the remaining mustard mixture. Sprinkle with the pecans.

Cover the dish with foil and bake for 20 minutes. Remove the foil and increase the temperature to 375°. Bake 10–15 minutes longer, until the chicken is cooked through. (Cut into one breast to make sure it's no longer pink inside.) If you want a little more browning on top, broil for about 5 minutes, watching very carefully to make sure the pecans and glaze don't burn.

Pecan-Stuffed Chicken Breasts

Boursin-style cheese is so handy to keep around. Either the herb flavor or the garlic flavor will work for this dish.

MAKES 4 SERVINGS

⅓ cup Boursin-style cheese
¼ cup toasted, chopped pecans
1 tablespoon chopped green onion tops
4 skinless, boneless chicken breasts
Salt and freshly ground black pepper
1 tablespoon unsalted butter
1 tablespoon vegetable oil

Combine the cheese, pecans, and green onions in a small bowl.
Place the chicken breasts on a work surface. Slide a knife
point horizontally along the thickest part of the breast, making
a pocket without cutting all the way through. Divide the cheese
and pecan mixture between the breasts, filling the pockets.
Bring the edges together and insert a toothpick through the
edges to hold the pocket closed. Sprinkle each breast with salt
and pepper.

Combine the butter and oil in a nonstick skillet over medium-
high heat until the butter is melted. Add the chicken, top-down.
Cook for 5–6 minutes on each side, turning carefully with tongs.
Remove from the pan. Cover and let stand for 1 minute before
serving.

Pecan Chicken Breasts with Dijon Cream Sauce

If you stop at a produce stand in North Florida or South Georgia, you may find bags of pecan meal for sale. Pecan meal is just finely ground pecans, which are used in this dish as an easy coating for chicken breasts. If you don't have pecan meal, pulse pecan halves in a food processor. Don't overprocess them or you'll end up with paste.

MAKES 4 SERVINGS

5 tablespoons unsalted butter, divided

3 tablespoons Dijon mustard, divided

1 cup pecan meal or finely ground pecans

2 tablespoons vegetable oil

4 skinless, boneless chicken breasts

½ cup coarsely chopped pecans

⅔ cup sour cream

½ teaspoon salt

¼ teaspoon freshly ground black pepper

Melt 3 tablespoons butter and place in a shallow dish, such as a pie plate. Whisk in 2 tablespoons mustard. Spread the pecan meal in another shallow dish.

Heat the remaining 2 tablespoons butter and the oil in a large nonstick skillet over medium heat until the butter is melted and just bubbling. Dip each chicken breast in the butter/Dijon mixture, then in the pecan meal, turning to coat both sides.

Place the chicken breasts in the skillet and cook for about 4 minutes over medium to medium-high heat, watching carefully so the crust doesn't burn. Turn with tongs and continue cooking about 4 minutes until cooked through (160° on an instant-read thermometer). Remove from the skillet to a serving platter.

Reduce the heat to low and stir in the coarsely chopped pecans. Cook for about 1 minute, then stir in the sour cream, remaining 1 tablespoon mustard, salt, and pepper. Blend until heated through and pour over the chicken breasts.

Pecan-Crusted Grouper

Thick, white-fleshed grouper is the perfect fish for this treatment, although you can substitute another fish, such as red snapper or tilapia.

MAKES 4 SERVINGS

$\frac{1}{4}$ cup pecan meal or finely ground pecans

$\frac{1}{4}$ cup panko crumbs

1 teaspoon Old Bay seasoning

$\frac{1}{2}$ teaspoon salt

$\frac{1}{4}$ teaspoon freshly ground black pepper

1–1$\frac{1}{2}$ pounds skin-on grouper fillets, cut into
   4-ounce servings

3 tablespoons vegetable oil, divided

3 tablespoons unsalted butter, divided

2–3 tablespoons minced shallot or mild white onion

$\frac{1}{4}$ cup white wine

1 tablespoon Dijon mustard

$\frac{1}{4}$ cup chopped pecans

Preheat the oven to 350°.

Combine the pecan meal, panko crumbs, Old Bay, salt, and pepper in a shallow dish, such as a pie plate.

Pat the fish fillets dry, then brush the flesh side with about 1 tablespoon oil. Place each fillet flesh-down in the pecan/crumb mixture and press lightly to coat.

Heat 1 tablespoon oil and 2 tablespoons butter in a nonstick ovenproof skillet over medium-high heat until the butter is melted and foaming. Place the fish in the skillet with the pecan coating down. Lower the heat to medium and cook for about 5 minutes.

Using tongs or a flat metal spatula, turn the fish skin-down, being careful not to dislodge the pecan coating. Place the skillet in the oven for 10–12 minutes, or until the fish is white and cooked through.

While the fish is baking, heat the remaining 1 tablespoon oil in a small saucepan and add the shallots. Cook for a few minutes, until the shallots are translucent. Add the wine, bring to a boil, and cook until reduced by half. Whisk in the mustard, then add the chopped pecans and remaining 1 tablespoon butter. Cook, stirring, until the butter is melted.

Remove the skillet from the oven. Place each fillet on a dinner plate and divide the sauce over the fillets.

Pecan-Stuffed Game Hens

This dish originated with the great French chef Pierre Franey, but I've changed it over the years as it became one of my favorite dishes for a romantic occasion. If I were remaking the lascivious dinner scene from the movie Tom Jones, *this is the dish I'd use. You can serve it for four in polite society or save it for two if you're looking for something that begs to be eaten with your fingers.*

MAKES 2–4 SERVINGS

½ cup finely minced pecans

6 tablespoons unsalted butter, at room temperature, divided

1 tablespoon Cognac or brandy

2 tablespoons Dijon mustard

2 Cornish game hens

4 russet potatoes

Salt and freshly ground black pepper

Preheat the oven to 450°.

Mix together the pecans, 4 tablespoons butter, brandy, and mustard. Slide your fingers under the skin over the breasts and thighs of the hens, making pockets. Push the butter mixture into the pockets, spreading it over the breasts and thighs. Use kitchen string to truss the hens, wrapping it around the legs and back around the wings, then tying it underneath.

Place the hens, breast up, in a roasting pan. Place the roasting pan in the oven for 10 minutes.

Peel the potatoes, dropping them in cold water until they're all peeled. Remove the potatoes from the water and slice thinly. Rinse the slices in hot water, then spread on paper towels and pat dry. Sprinkle with salt and pepper.

Remove the roasting pan from the oven and arrange the potato slices around the hens. Dot with the remaining 2 tablespoons butter, cut into pieces. Bake for 10 minutes.

Turn the hens breast-down, using tongs. Roast for 15 minutes. Turn them breast up again and roast for 10 minutes. Remove the roasting pan from the oven and let stand for 5 minutes.

Place the hens on a cutting board, cut away the string, and cut each hen in half. Place on a serving platter, cut-side down. Use a metal spatula to remove the potato slices to the platter (some will be brown and crisp, some will be lighter and softer).

Honey-Pecan Chicken Thighs

You could use other cuts of chicken for this dish, but chicken thighs are just so darn delicious. They're truly the tastiest part of the bird.

MAKES 4–6 SERVINGS

2 teaspoons olive oil
6 skin-on, bone-in chicken thighs
½ cup cider vinegar
½ cup honey
1 teaspoon cayenne pepper
2 teaspoons cornstarch
1 teaspoon salt
½ cup chopped pecans

Preheat the oven to 375°.

Warm the olive oil in a nonstick skillet over medium-high heat. Place the chicken thighs in the skillet skin-down. Cook for about 8 minutes, until the skin is browned. Turn and cook for about 3 minutes. Remove the thighs from the skillet with tongs and place in a baking dish large enough to hold them in a single layer.

Reduce the heat to medium. Add the vinegar, honey, and cayenne to the skillet, stirring up any browned bits, and simmer for 2–3 minutes.

Combine the cornstarch with 2 tablespoons water in a small dish, stirring to completely dissolve the cornstarch. Stir the cornstarch and water into the sauce in the skillet, cooking for 2–3 minutes until thickened. Add the salt and pecans. Pour the sauce over the thighs in the baking dish.

Bake for 15 minutes, then spoon the sauce and pecans over the chicken thighs to glaze. Continue baking for 15 minutes, or until the thighs are done.

Salads and Sides

Pecans are definitely not limited to desserts. In the spring and summer, they pair with fruits and fresh greens in salads. In the fall and winter, they bring a luxurious touch to roasted vegetables. At Thanksgiving, I have to double-check my menu to make sure I haven't used them in every dish.

When you're adding pecans to a dish, remember that a 1-ounce serving (18–19 halves) has 200 calories, 20 grams of fat (2 grams saturated, 18 grams unsaturated), 0 cholesterol, 0 sodium, 116 milligrams of potassium, 4 grams of carbohydrates, and 3 grams of protein.

Strawberry Spinach Salad with Pecans

"What grows together, goes together" is one of the great kitchen lessons. When fresh strawberries are at their best in the spring, tender spinach is usually still in the fields, too. Add pecans for crunch, and you have a tasty salad. This recipe will make more dressing than you need for the salad, so you can cover and refrigerate it to use later.

MAKES 4–6 SERVINGS

½ cup pecan halves
½ medium onion, sliced
About 6 cups fresh spinach
2 cups strawberries
¼ cup fresh goat cheese, crumbled
1 medium orange
¼ teaspoon salt
1 teaspoon dry mustard
2 tablespoons apple cider vinegar
½ cup extra-virgin olive oil
1 teaspoon poppy seeds

Spread the pecans in a dry skillet over medium heat and toast, stirring often, until fragrant. Cool and chop coarsely.

Place the onion in a small bowl. Cover with cold water and let stand.

Wash the spinach well and spin dry. Remove the thick stems and tear the leaves into bite-sized pieces. Place in a large salad bowl.

Remove the hulls (the leafy stem section) from the strawberries with the tip of a paring knife. Slice the strawberries and add to the spinach with the pecans. Drain the onion well and add to the salad with the goat cheese. Toss well. Grate the orange zest and sprinkle over the salad.

Squeeze the juice from the orange into a small bowl (you should have about ½ cup). Whisk in the salt, dry mustard, and vinegar. Whisking constantly, slowly drizzle in the oil. Stir in the poppy seeds.

Add just enough dressing to the salad to moisten and toss well. Serve immediately.

Pecan Vinaigrette

Bonus: You get a powerfully flavored dressing that's great on strong-tasting greens, such as arugula or spinach. And the chunks of pecans add another texture to your salad. If you don't have sherry vinegar, try a wine vinegar. Balsamic would be too strong.

MAKES ABOUT ¾ CUP

¼ cup chopped pecans
2 tablespoons sherry vinegar
2 teaspoons honey
1 teaspoon Dijon mustard
1 teaspoon minced fresh thyme
4 tablespoons olive oil

Spread the pecans in a dry skillet over medium heat. Heat, stirring frequently, just until fragrant and barely toasted. Remove from the heat.

Combine the vinegar, honey, mustard, and thyme in a small bowl. Whisking constantly, slowly drizzle in the oil to create a creamy dressing.

Pour the dressing into the skillet with the pecans. Place over medium heat and cook, stirring, until heated through. Cool before tossing with the salad.

Pecan Waldorf Salad

Waldorf Salad is so easy to make from things you can keep on hand that it appears regularly on my dinner table. Toasting the pecans to bring out their flavor and cutting the mayonnaise with plain yogurt helps reduce the fat.

MAKES 4 SERVINGS

½ cup coarsely chopped pecans
2 medium red apples, cut into large dice, skin-on
1–2 stalks celery, diced
¼ cup mayonnaise
¼ cup plain nonfat yogurt, preferably Greek-style
½ teaspoon celery seed
½ teaspoon salt

Place the pecans in a small, dry skillet over medium to medium-low heat and toast, stirring often, until fragrant. Watch carefully so they don't burn. Cool.

In a large bowl, mix together the apples and celery. Add the pecans, mayonnaise, yogurt, celery seed, and salt. Mix well. Serve chilled or at room temperature. Can be made up to 24 hours in advance, covered well, and refrigerated.

Cornbread Dressing with Pecans and Apples

Like many southerners, I bake dressing separately from a chicken or turkey (and yes, I call it dressing instead of stuffing). But you could use it to stuff a bird if you prefer. Cornbread dressing that is all cornbread can be heavy and a bit gritty. Get the best of both worlds by combining equal amounts of crumbled cornbread and cubes of sourdough bread.

MAKES 8 SERVINGS

Nonstick cooking spray
4–6 cups crumbled cornbread (about 1 8-inch square)
4–6 cups crusty sourdough bread, cut into small cubes
     (about ⅓–½ loaf)
2 tablespoons olive oil
2 tablespoons unsalted butter
1 cup chopped onion
½ cup diced celery
1 cup coarsely chopped pecans
½ red apple, diced, skin-on
1 pound pork breakfast sausage
2 large eggs, lightly beaten
3–4 cups chicken stock
1 tablespoon dried, rubbed sage
1 teaspoon dried marjoram
1 teaspoon dried thyme
2 teaspoons salt
½ teaspoon freshly ground black pepper

Preheat the oven to 375°. Spray a 13 × 9-inch baking dish with nonstick cooking spray.

In a large mixing bowl, combine the cornbread and sourdough bread and toss to mix well.

Heat the olive oil and butter in a skillet over medium heat. Add the onion and cook for about 5 minutes, stirring often. Add the celery and continue cooking for about 5 minutes, until the onion is getting soft and the celery is just losing its crunch. Stir in the pecans and cook for a couple of minutes, until fragrant. Remove from the heat and stir into the cornbread mixture along with the apple.

Brown the sausage in the skillet, crumbling it as it cooks. Spread on a paper towel to drain, then stir into the cornbread mixture.

Stir in the eggs and enough chicken stock to make the mixture very moist. (It may seem a little too wet, but that's OK. Dressing needs to be very moist when it goes into the oven.) Add the sage, marjoram, thyme, salt, and pepper. Turn the mixture into the prepared baking dish.

Cover with foil and bake for about 45 minutes. Remove the foil and add a little broth (or drippings from a roasting chicken or turkey) if it looks dry. Continue baking for about 15 minutes, until the top is starting to get crunchy.

Bourbon–Sweet Potato Casserole with Pecans

It may be possible to serve a Thanksgiving meal without sweet potatoes, but it would be wrong. Call them yams if you must, but skip the marshmallows and top them with a crunchy coating of pecans.

MAKES 8 SERVINGS

3–4 pounds sweet potatoes
6 tablespoons unsalted butter, divided
2 tablespoons heavy cream
3 tablespoons bourbon
1¼ cups packed light brown sugar, divided
½ teaspoon ground cinnamon
½ teaspoon salt
¼ teaspoon freshly grated nutmeg
¼ teaspoon ground allspice
⅓ cup all-purpose flour
1 cup chopped pecans

Preheat the oven to 350°.

Scrub the sweet potatoes well. Place on a baking sheet and bake for about 1 hour, until very soft when you press the skins. Remove from the oven and let stand until cool enough to handle. Slice in half and scoop the flesh into a large mixing bowl, discarding the skins.

Beat the sweet potatoes with a wooden spoon or heavy whisk to mash them well. Stir in 2 tablespoons butter, the cream, the bourbon, and ¼ cup brown sugar. Beat in the cinnamon, salt, nutmeg, and allspice. Spread in a 1½-quart baking dish.

In a small bowl, combine the remaining 1 cup brown sugar and flour. Cut in the remaining 4 tablespoons butter, using a pastry blender or a fork to blend well. Stir in the chopped pecans. Sprinkle the topping over the sweet potatoes. (Can be made ahead to this point and refrigerated for up to 24 hours. Bring to room temperature before baking.)

Bake for 30 minutes, until the topping is light brown and a little crisp and the casserole is bubbly.

Broccoli-Pecan Salad

I love taking this colorful, crunchy salad to potlucks or putting it out on a buffet. It always disappears quickly.

MAKES 4–6 SERVINGS

1 small head broccoli, cut into florets (save stalks for
   another use)
¼ cup dried cranberries or dried cherries
½ medium red onion, minced
½ cup toasted, chopped pecans
4 tablespoons reduced-fat mayonnaise
2 tablespoons sugar
2 tablespoons nonfat milk
2 teaspoons cider vinegar
¼ teaspoon salt

Toss the broccoli, cranberries, onion, and pecans in a large serving bowl. Whisk together the mayonnaise, sugar, milk, vinegar, and salt in a small bowl. Pour over the salad and toss to mix well. Cover and refrigerate for at least 30 minutes before serving.

Fresh Cranberry Relish

Forget the canned cranberry sauce. This fresh sweet/tart version is so much brighter and livelier. It's a welcome touch on a Thanksgiving table loaded with heavy flavors. And in the middle of putting together a holiday dinner, it's a relief to have something made in advance and tucked away in the refrigerator.

MAKES 8 SERVINGS

---

1 (12-ounce) bag fresh cranberries
2 small oranges or 1 medium orange
1½ cups sugar
1 cup coarsely chopped pecans

Place the cranberries in a sieve and wash under cold water. Pick over the berries, discarding any soft ones and any small stems.

Wash the oranges. Slice off the ends and discard. Cut into wedges, leaving the peel on. Cut away any excess pith from the edges and pick out any seeds.

Place the cranberries and orange wedges (yes, peel-on) in a food processor. Pulse several times to chop coarsely. Scrape into a bowl. Stir in the sugar and pecans. Refrigerate for up to 24 hours before serving.

Roasted Broccoli with Browned Butter Pecan Sauce

You can substitute Brussels sprouts for the broccoli. Cut the little heads in half and roast them the same way.

MAKES 4 SERVINGS

---

1 large head broccoli
1 tablespoon olive oil
1 teaspoon kosher salt
4 tablespoons unsalted butter
2 teaspoons minced garlic
1 tablespoon Dijon mustard
1 teaspoon fresh lemon juice
¼ cup chopped pecans

Preheat the oven to 350°.

Trim the stalk from the broccoli. Cut away any tough bits and slice the stalk into thin coins. Cut the florets into slices to create lots of flat sides.

Place the broccoli in a large roasting pan or rimmed baking sheet. Drizzle with the oil, stirring to coat. Spread it all out with as many flat sides down as possible. Sprinkle with the salt.

Place in the oven and roast for about 30 minutes, stirring once or twice, until the flat sides are a little brown and the broccoli is tender.

While the broccoli is roasting, make the sauce. Place the butter in a small saucepan or skillet over medium heat. As it melts, the butter will crackle as the water cooks away. Just as it starts to brown, add the garlic and reduce the heat to medium-low. Stir and cook a minute or two, just until the garlic is very fragrant. Stir in the mustard and lemon juice, mixing well, then stir in the pecans. Heat for about 2 minutes.

Remove the broccoli from the oven and pour into a serving bowl. Add the sauce and toss to mix well.

Desserts

Pecan pie and pralines are just the beginning. Once you start coming up with recipes for cookies and candies with pecans, it's hard to stop. Butter and brown sugar almost seem like they were created to use with pecans.

Of course, the most classic pecan dessert of all is pecan pie. But not everyone is a fan. I found this passage by Florida author Marjorie Kinnan Rawlings in her cookbook *Cross Creek Cookery* (1942):

> True Southern pecan pie is one of the richest, most deadly desserts of my knowledge. It is more overpowering than English treacle pie, which it resembles in texture, for to the insult of the cooked-down syrup is added the injury of the rich pecan meats. It is a favorite with folk who have a sweet tooth, and fat men in particular are addicted to it. I have nibbled at the Utterly Deadly Southern Pecan Pie, and have served it to those in whose welfare I took no interest, but being inclined to plumpness, and having as well a desire to see out my days on earth, I have never eaten a full portion.

I can't say I have Ms. Rawlings's restraint, and my waistline is proof.

Classic Southern Pecan Pie

Recipes for pecan pie range widely in the type of sweetener and the amount of butter and eggs used. I went through a half-dozen experiments before settling on what I think is the definitive version.

MAKES 8 SERVINGS

---

1 9-inch piecrust, unbaked (see Note below)

1½ cups pecan halves

3 large eggs

1 cup packed light brown sugar

1 cup light corn syrup

1 teaspoon vanilla

½ teaspoon salt

2 tablespoons melted unsalted butter

Preheat the oven to 350°. Dust a pie plate with flour and add the piecrust, easing into the bottom. Turn the edge under and crimp to create a border.

Spread the pecans evenly in the bottom of the crust. Whisk the eggs in a medium bowl, then whisk in the brown sugar, corn syrup, vanilla, salt, and melted butter. Pour over the pecans in the crust.

Bake for 55–60 minutes. (If the edges are browning too fast, place strips of foil over them.) Remove from the oven and cool completely before cutting. Refrigerate leftovers.

NOTE ✳ If you use a refrigerated piecrust (and who doesn't sometimes?), dust a work surface and a rolling pin with flour and roll out the crust slightly thinner. That will flatten the wrinkled edges and make the crust taste more like homemade.

Crispy Pecan Pie

Many old southern recipes add cornmeal to pecan pie filling. It gives a consistency that is a little less gooey and lets the pecans stand out a bit more.

MAKES 8 SERVINGS

1 9-inch piecrust, unbaked
1½ cups pecan halves
2 large eggs
1 cup packed light brown sugar
1 tablespoon yellow or white cornmeal
1 tablespoon water
2 teaspoons vanilla
½ teaspoon salt
4 tablespoons melted unsalted butter

Preheat the oven to 375°. Dust a pie plate with flour and add the piecrust, easing into the bottom. Turn the edge under and crimp to create a border.

Spread the pecan halves evenly in the bottom of the crust. Whisk together the eggs, brown sugar, cornmeal, water, vanilla, salt, and melted butter. Pour over the pecans in the crust, spreading to cover them completely.

Bake for 15 minutes. Reduce the heat to 350° and continue baking for 30 minutes. Remove from the oven and cool completely before cutting. Refrigerate leftovers.

Pecan Cream Pie

My friend Catherine Rabb wears a lot of hats. She and her husband own the Charlotte restaurant Fenwick's, where Catherine is both chef and wine expert. This pie is one of the house specialties.

MAKES 8 SERVINGS

1 9-inch piecrust, unbaked
1 (8-ounce) package cream cheese, at room temperature
1½ cups sugar, divided
4 large eggs, divided
1 teaspoon vanilla
1½ cups pecan halves
1 cup light corn syrup

Place an oven rack in the center position and make sure there is no rack above it. (The pie puffs up while it bakes, so it needs plenty of clearance to avoid sticking to the rack above it.) Preheat the oven to 350°. Dust a pie plate with flour and add the piecrust, easing into the bottom. Turn the edge under and crimp to create a border.

Beat the cream cheese, ¾ cup sugar, 1 egg, and vanilla with an electric mixer. Don't overbeat: The mixture should be well mixed but not too fluffy because it has to hold up the remaining layers. Spread evenly on the piecrust, then sprinkle the pecans evenly over the cream cheese layer.

Beat together the remaining 3 eggs, the remaining ¾ cup sugar, and the corn syrup. Pour over the pecan layer.

Bake for 45 minutes, until golden brown and fairly firm (the center may still be a little jiggly). Cool completely and chill for at least 2 hours before cutting. The pie keeps refrigerated for several days but can't be frozen.

Chocolate-Maple Pecan Pie

This pie is not quite as sweet as the South's traditional corn syrup pie, and it has a touch of semisweet chocolate to cut the maple syrup. Grade B syrup isn't as fine as Grade A, but I think it has a more emphatic maple flavor.

MAKES 8 SERVINGS

1 9-inch piecrust, unbaked
4 large eggs
½ cup sugar
4 tablespoons melted unsalted butter
⅔ cup plus ¼ cup maple syrup, preferably Grade B
1 teaspoon vanilla
1 cup pecan halves
¼ cup semisweet chocolate chips or chopped dark chocolate
1 cup whipping cream

Preheat the oven to 400°. Dust a pie plate with flour and add the piecrust, easing into the bottom. Turn the edge under and crimp to create a border.

Beat the eggs and sugar with an electric mixer. With the mixer running, drizzle in the melted butter, then ⅔ cup maple syrup and the vanilla. Fold in the pecans and chocolate. Pour into the piecrust.

Bake for 20 minutes, then reduce the heat to 350°. (Place a shield of foil around the rim of the crust if it's getting too brown.) Bake for 15–18 minutes, until just barely set and still a little jiggly in the middle. Remove from the oven and cool on a rack.

Beat the whipping cream with the remaining ¼ cup maple syrup. Slice the pie and serve each piece with a dollop of maple whipped cream.

Chocolate Praline Cheesecake

For the crust of this cheesecake, don't look for chocolate wafer cookies on the cookie aisle. Most stores stock them on the ice cream aisle. They're the cookie used to make the classic chocolate wafer icebox cake.

MAKES 12 SERVINGS

FOR THE CRUST

Half of a (9-ounce) package chocolate wafer cookies
½ cup confectioners' sugar
1 stick melted unsalted butter

FOR THE CAKE

2 tablespoons unsalted butter
1 cup coarsely chopped pecans, plus 12–14 pecan halves
    for garnish
2 (8-ounce) packages cream cheese, at room temperature
1 cup packed light brown sugar
⅓ cup unsweetened cocoa
3 large eggs
1 teaspoon vanilla
½ teaspoon salt

To make the crust, preheat the oven to 350°. Place the chocolate wafers in a resealable freezer bag and beat with a mallet or rolling pin to make fine crumbs. You should have about 1½ cups. Combine the crumbs with the confectioners' sugar and melted butter. Press into the bottom and about an inch up the side of a 9-inch nonstick springform pan. Bake for 8 minutes. Remove from the oven to cool and increase the oven temperature to 400°.

To make the cheesecake, while the crust is baking, melt the butter in a small skillet and add the chopped pecans. Sauté lightly for about 5 minutes, until very fragrant. Spread the pecans on a paper towel to drain.

Beat the cream cheese and brown sugar with an electric mixer until very light and fluffy. Beat in the cocoa on low speed. Add the eggs one at a time, beating well after each. Beat in the vanilla and salt. Stir in the sautéed pecans with a rubber spatula, making sure the batter is well combined.

Pour into the baked chocolate crust. Bake for 10 minutes. Reduce the heat to 300° and continue baking for 45 minutes, until the cheesecake is set but still a little jiggly in the middle. Remove from the oven and let stand for about 10 minutes. Press the pecan halves around the top edge of the cheesecake.

Refrigerate for at least 6 hours or overnight. Run a knife around the inside of the rim, release the springform ring, and carefully remove. Use a spatula to separate the cake from the pan bottom and slide the cake onto a serving plate.

Pecan Meringue Bites

Making the long drive through Florida on I-95, you see the bill-boards over and over: "Papershell Pecans, This Exit." Passing the time on one trip, I started thinking about adding pecans to meringue cookies that are sometimes called Forgotten Cookies because you turn off the oven and leave them overnight. Then I started thinking about Pavlova, that great crispy meringue with the chewy middle. That led to this idea, a meltingly crispy pecan treat with a hint of caramel flavor.

MAKES ABOUT 30 SMALL COOKIES

2 large egg whites

2 tablespoons packed light brown sugar

$\frac{1}{2}$ cup granulated sugar

$\frac{1}{8}$ teaspoon salt

$\frac{1}{2}$ teaspoon vanilla

$\frac{1}{2}$ cup coarsely chopped pecans

1 teaspoon cornstarch

$\frac{1}{2}$ teaspoon white vinegar

Preheat the oven to 350°. Line 1 or 2 baking sheets with parchment paper or nonstick foil.

Beat the egg whites with an electric mixer until they form stiff peaks when the beaters are lifted. Beat in the brown sugar and granulated sugar a tablespoon at a time. Beat in the salt and vanilla.

Sprinkle the pecans, cornstarch, and vinegar over the beaten egg-white mixture. Fold in gently but thoroughly with a rubber spatula.

Using a teaspoon, spoon the batter onto the lined baking sheets. (Don't worry about getting the cookies too close together—they won't spread much.)

Place the baking sheets in the oven. Turn off the oven and leave them in the oven with the door closed for 8–12 hours or overnight. Peel the cookies off the parchment or foil and store in an airtight container.

Crispy Pecan Chocolate Chip Cookies

Soft cookies are nice, but crispness really brings out the buttery caramel flavor. Besides having an unholy amount of butter, this recipe employs a couple of tricks to increase the crunch: using both white and dark brown sugar, and letting the sugar and butter sit for a while so the sugar melts a little before the cookies go in the oven. It also has just a bit more salt, which brings out the pecan flavor.

MAKES 5–6 DOZEN COOKIES

Nonstick cooking spray

3 sticks unsalted butter, at room temperature

1 cup granulated sugar

3/4 cup packed dark brown sugar

2 large eggs, at room temperature

1 1/2 teaspoons vanilla

3 cups all-purpose flour

1 1/2 teaspoons salt

1 teaspoon baking soda

1 (12-ounce) bag semisweet chocolate chips

1 1/2 cups chopped pecans

Place two oven racks in the upper and center positions. Preheat the oven to 375°. Spray 2 baking sheets with nonstick cooking spray.

Beat the butter and both sugars on high speed with an electric mixer until light and fluffy, about 1 minute. Scrape down the bowl and beater. Add the eggs and vanilla. Beat on low until blended, then raise the speed to high and beat for 1 minute. Turn off the mixer and let stand for 10 minutes.

Whisk together the flour, salt, and baking soda in a separate bowl. Beat into the butter mixture in several additions on medium-low just until blended. Fold in the chocolate chips and pecans with a wooden spoon or rubber spatula.

Drop the dough onto the prepared baking sheets by rounded teaspoon, allowing 2 inches between cookies. Place the baking sheets on the two racks in the oven and bake for 9–10 minutes, swapping shelves after 5 minutes. Remove the baking sheets from the oven and let stand a minute or two. Use a spatula to move the cookies to a cooling rack. Store in an airtight container for several days.

World's Greatest Pecan Cookies

There are a number of versions of this recipe. I upped the pecan quotient, making them even better. The cookies are deceptive: Since they are pale and not crammed with chocolate, people never expect them to be as delicious as they are.

MAKES ABOUT 6 DOZEN COOKIES

1 cup quick-cooking or old-fashioned oatmeal (not instant)

1 cup puffed rice cereal, such as Rice Krispies

1 cup frozen coconut, thawed

1½ cups pecan halves, divided

3½ cups all-purpose flour

1 teaspoon baking soda

1 teaspoon salt

2 sticks unsalted butter, at room temperature

1 cup packed light brown sugar

1 cup granulated sugar

1 large egg

1 cup vegetable oil

1 teaspoon almond extract

Preheat the oven to 325°.

Combine the oatmeal, cereal, and coconut and ½ cup pecans in a blender or food processor. Pulse until finely ground. Coarsely chop the remaining 1 cup pecans. Stir into the ground mixture.

Combine the flour, baking soda, and salt in a separate bowl. Mix until blended.

Beat the butter, brown sugar, and granulated sugar in a large bowl with an electric mixer until fluffy. Add the egg and mix until well blended. Beat in the oil and almond extract. Stir in the oatmeal and pecan mixture with a rubber spatula or wooden spoon. Stir in the flour mixture until the dough is very smooth.

Drop by teaspoon about 1 ½ inches apart on an ungreased baking sheet. Dip a fork into a glass of water and make crisscross patterns on top of the cookies to flatten them a little.

Bake for 12–15 minutes, until the cookies are brown around the edges. Cool on the baking sheet for a minute or two, then remove to a cooling rack with a flat metal spatula. Cool completely. Store in an airtight container. Cookies also keep well frozen.

Pecan Tassies

These bite-sized pecan treats that look like tiny pecan pies always turn up on tea tables around Christmas. This version uses a cream cheese dough for a soft, tender base, like a soft cookie cup with a rich filling. The sprinkling of crispy sea salt adds a touch of sophistication. You'll need a mini-muffin pan, sometimes called a gem pan.

MAKES ABOUT 3 DOZEN TASSIES

1 (8-ounce) package cream cheese, at room temperature

2 sticks unsalted butter, at room temperature

2½ cups sifted all-purpose flour (sift, then measure)

2 large eggs

1½ cups packed light brown sugar

2 tablespoons melted unsalted butter

¼ teaspoon table salt

1 teaspoon vanilla

1 cup coarsely chopped pecans

Crispy sea salt, preferably Maldon's

Beat the cream cheese and butter in a large bowl with an electric mixer until fluffy. With the mixer on low, beat in the flour in several additions. Beat just until the dough starts to come together. Scrape the dough onto a sheet of plastic wrap, making sure to get all the crumbly bits from the bottom of the bowl. Press together into a ball, wrap, and chill for at least 1 hour.

Beat the eggs in a mixing bowl with an electric mixer. Add the brown sugar, melted butter, table salt, and vanilla. Beat until well blended.

Preheat the oven to 325°.

Remove the dough from the refrigerator. Break off pieces of dough and roll into balls about 1½–2 inches in diameter. Place each ball of dough into a cup of a mini-muffin pan. Press your thumb into the dough, then press the dough up the sides of the cup and a little over the edge. After you've filled all the cups with dough, sprinkle several pecan pieces in the bottom of each cup. Spoon in about 1 teaspoon of the batter, then sprinkle with a little bit of sea salt and a few more pecan pieces. Return the remaining dough to the refrigerator.

Bake for 25 minutes. Run a table knife around each tassy and remove from the pan. Cool on a wire rack. Repeat with the remaining dough. Store in an airtight container for 2–3 days.

NOTE ✳ Make sure you stir the filling as you go along because the sugar will settle as it sits.

Pecan Lace Cookies

Lace cookies are sometimes called Florentines, but the oatmeal makes this version a bit sturdier. I based this recipe on one made by the best cook I've ever known, my late aunt Rosalie Bass of Americus, Georgia.

MAKES ABOUT 3 DOZEN COOKIES

1 stick unsalted butter

1 cup sugar

$\frac{1}{2}$ teaspoon salt

1 cup quick-cooking or old-fashioned oatmeal (not instant)

1 large egg

$\frac{1}{4}$ teaspoon baking powder

3 tablespoons all-purpose flour

1 teaspoon vanilla

$\frac{1}{4}$ cup coconut (frozen and thawed or sweetened, flaked is fine)

$\frac{1}{2}$ cup coarsely chopped pecans

Preheat the oven to 375°. Cover a baking sheet with aluminum foil (see Note below).

Melt the butter in a large saucepan over medium heat. Remove from the heat and stir in the remaining ingredients. (The batter should be soft.)

Drop the batter by teaspoon at least 3 inches apart on the prepared baking sheet. Flatten each cookie a little with the back of the spoon.

Bake for about 8 minutes, until each cookie is brown around the edges. (Watch carefully so they don't burn.) Remove the sheet of foil with the cookies and place on a wire rack to cool. Place another sheet of foil on the baking sheet and spoon out the remaining batter.

Cool the cookies completely, then peel off the foil. (If they seem to be sticking in the center, they aren't cool enough.) Store in an airtight container.

NOTE ❋ When you cover the pan with foil, use a single sheet even if it doesn't completely cover the pan. Don't overlap sheets or the batter may creep under the edge and you'll end up with a cookie that has foil baked into it. Make sure you have enough foil for two batches.

Pecan Toffee

Every year at Christmas, my mother would continue her search for the perfect English toffee recipe, always forgetting which recipe she had used the year before. So some years we had soft toffee and some years we had crunchy toffee. No matter—I developed such an addiction to it that it is still my single most favorite thing to eat. You'll need a candy thermometer.

MAKES ABOUT 30 PIECES

1 cup pecan halves

2 sticks unsalted butter, plus more for preparing the pan

1 cup sugar

2 teaspoons light corn syrup

1 teaspoon kosher salt

1 teaspoon vanilla

8 ounces semisweet chocolate chips or chopped dark chocolate

Butter a rimmed baking sheet.

Spread the pecans in a dry skillet and toast over medium heat until fragrant. Remove from the heat and chop coarsely.

Place a small bowl of water and a brush beside the stove. In a heavy saucepan, combine the butter, sugar, corn syrup, and salt. Place over medium heat and cook, stirring, until the butter is melted and the sugar is dissolved. Attach a candy thermometer to the side of the pan, making sure the bulb isn't touching the bottom.

Bring the sugar to a boil, occasionally brushing down the inside of the pan with water to keep it clear of sugar crystals. Stir regularly but not constantly, especially as brown areas begin to develop in the sugar.

Cook until the sugar reaches 300–310°, or the hard-crack stage, about 20 minutes. Remove from the heat and stir in the vanilla.

Immediately pour the toffee onto the prepared pan, tilting the pan a little to spread it out into a pool about ½-inch thick. (It won't reach the edges of the pan, but you want it to spread a little so it isn't too thick in the middle.) Let stand for 3–5 minutes.

Sprinkle the chocolate over the still-warm toffee. Let stand for 1 minute to soften, then spread it out using a knife or an offset spatula. Immediately sprinkle the chopped pecans over the chocolate, pressing them into the chocolate. Let stand for several hours or refrigerate for 1 hour. Lift the toffee from the sheet and break into pieces. Store in a covered container in the refrigerator to keep the chocolate firm.

Leche Quemada

Sweetened condensed milk is a popular ingredient in Brazil. "Leche quemada" means "burned milk," but this isn't burned. It's an easy microwave candy with a vanilla fudge texture and a creamy flavor that lets the pecans really stand out. If you're intimidated by candy thermometers and boiling sugar mixtures, this is the candy for you.

MAKES ABOUT 3 DOZEN PIECES

2 cups chopped pecans
1 stick unsalted butter, plus more for preparing the dish
$2/3$ cup packed light brown sugar
1 (14-ounce) can sweetened condensed milk
1 teaspoon vanilla
$1/2$ teaspoon salt

Butter an 8-inch square pan.

Spread the pecans in a dry skillet and toast over medium heat, stirring often, until fragrant.

Place the butter in a heavy microwave-safe bowl that's deep enough so the sugar mixture has room to bubble up (a 3-quart glass mixing bowl is a good choice). Microwave on high in 30-second bursts until melted.

Stir in the brown sugar and sweetened condensed milk. Microwave on high for 2 minutes. Remove the bowl and stir with a wooden spoon. (Be careful—as the sugar begins to boil, the bowl will get hot.) Microwave for 1 minute, then stir again. Continue microwaving for 1 minute and then stirring for a total of 6–7 minutes, until the sugar is completely dissolved. (To check, spread a little onto a glass plate. It should be thick enough to leave a track when you draw a spoon through it.)

Immediately begin beating with a wooden spoon for about 5 minutes, until the sugar thickens and loses its gloss. Beat in the vanilla, salt, and pecans. Quickly spread in the prepared pan. Refrigerate until firm and cut into squares. Store in the refrigerator.

Coconut-Pecan Dessert Bars

Everyone needs a drop-dead simple bar cookie for last-minute bake sales and potlucks. This one is made from things you probably have on hand and is ready in less than an hour (although it cuts easier if you chill it overnight).

MAKES ABOUT 16 BARS

Nonstick cooking spray
$\frac{1}{2}$ cup melted unsalted butter
$1\frac{1}{2}$ cups fine graham cracker crumbs
$\frac{1}{2}$ cup sugar
1 cup semisweet chocolate chips
1 cup butterscotch chips
1 cup sweetened, flaked coconut
1 cup chopped pecans
1 (14-ounce) can sweetened condensed milk

Preheat the oven to 350°. Spray a 13 × 9-inch glass baking dish with nonstick cooking spray.

In a mixing bowl, combine the melted butter, graham crackers, and sugar and stir until the crumbs are completely moistened. Press the crumbs into the bottom of the baking dish. Bake for 8 minutes. Remove from the oven.

Sprinkle the chocolate chips, butterscotch chips, coconut, and pecans evenly over the crust. Pour the sweetened condensed milk over the top. (Don't worry if there are gaps; it will spread as it bakes.)

Return to the oven and bake for 30 minutes. Cool. Chill for 1 hour or overnight before cutting.

Pecan Pralines

Is it any wonder that pralines are a classic of both New Orleans and Charleston? The texture and the flavor are simply irresistible. As long as you have a candy thermometer and a strong arm for beating, pralines aren't difficult to make. But don't attempt making them on a rainy day. They may not set up properly.

MAKES ABOUT 2 DOZEN, DEPENDING ON THE SIZE

Nonstick cooking spray
1 (16-ounce) box light brown sugar
¼ cup granulated sugar
6 tablespoons unsalted butter
2 cups coarsely chopped pecans
1 cup heavy cream

Spread out a large sheet of parchment paper and spray with nonstick cooking spray.

Combine all ingredients in a large, heavy pot over medium-high heat. Stir until the butter is melted and the mixture comes to a full, rolling boil. Attach a candy thermometer to the side of the pot, making sure the bulb isn't touching the bottom. Cook until the mixture reaches 240°. Remove from the heat and let stand for 5 minutes.

Beat vigorously with a wooden spoon until the mixture thickens and is just starting to pull together. Immediately drop the pralines by tablespoon onto the prepared parchment paper. Let stand until set. Store in an airtight container for up to 3 days.

NOTE ❋ Knowing when to stop beating is the trickiest part of making pralines. The mixture should still be a little shiny and soft enough to spoon out but firm enough to hold its shape. Some sources say it will change color when it's ready, but the change can be very subtle.

Baked Pecan Toffee

This doesn't have the intense butter flavor of crunchy English toffee, but it's an easy candy to make when you need something fast for a bake sale or to fill up a holiday cookie basket.

MAKES ABOUT 5 DOZEN PIECES

---

2 sticks unsalted butter, plus more for preparing the pan
1 cup packed light brown sugar
½ teaspoon salt
2½ cups finely chopped pecans, divided
1½ cups semisweet chocolate chips

Preheat the oven to 375°. Lightly butter a 13 × 9-inch baking pan.

Place the butter, brown sugar, and salt in a large, heavy saucepan over medium heat. Cook, stirring, until the butter melts. Heat until the mixture comes to a full, active boil, with bubbles that don't disappear when you stir. (Don't raise the heat or you'll risk burning it. Just be patient.)

Remove from the heat and stir in 2 cups pecans. Pour into the prepared pan and bake for 15 minutes.

Remove from the oven and let stand for a minute or two, until the sugar stops bubbling vigorously. Sprinkle the chocolate chips over the hot toffee and let stand briefly, until the chocolate softens. Spread the chocolate evenly with an offset spatula. Sprinkle with the remaining ½ cup pecans.

Chill until completely firm. Break into pieces. Store in an airtight container.

Pecan Penuche

Penuche is like a caramel-flavored fudge. If you spread it while it's soft, it can double as a decadently rich cake icing.

MAKES ABOUT 16 PIECES

1 stick unsalted butter, plus more for preparing the pan
1 cup packed light brown sugar
1/4 cup milk
1 3/4–2 cups confectioners' sugar
1/2 cup chopped pecans

Butter an 8-inch square pan.

Heat the butter in a medium saucepan over medium-low heat until mostly melted. Add the brown sugar and cook, stirring, for 2 minutes. Stir in the milk. Increase the heat to medium and continue to cook, stirring, until it comes to a boil that you can't stir down.

Remove from the heat and cool for 5 minutes. Using a sifter or sieve held over the saucepan, gradually beat in the confectioners' sugar with a wooden spoon, adding sugar until the candy lightens in color and thickens to a fudgey but still soft consistency.

Stir in the pecans and spread the candy in the prepared pan. Chill until firm. Cut into small squares. Store in an airtight container.

Southern Pecan Ice Cream

Cane syrup and buttered, salted pecans give this ice cream a haunting richness. Any cane syrup will do, although my favorite is Steen's from Louisiana. If you don't have cane syrup, you could use good-quality maple syrup, but the flavor will be much milder.

MAKES 1 QUART

2 tablespoons unsalted butter

2 cups coarsely chopped pecans

1 teaspoon kosher salt or $\frac{1}{2}$ teaspoon table salt

1 tablespoon sugar

$1\frac{1}{2}$ teaspoons cornstarch

1 large egg

1 cup milk

$\frac{1}{2}$ cup cane syrup

$2\frac{1}{2}$ cups heavy cream

Melt the butter in a skillet over medium heat and add the pecans and salt. Cook, stirring often, until the pecans are fragrant and a little toasted. (Watch carefully so they don't burn.) Remove from the skillet and spread on paper towels to drain.

Stir together the sugar and cornstarch in a small saucepan. Whisk in the egg, making sure to incorporate all the sugar mixture. Whisk in the milk.

Place over medium heat and cook, stirring constantly, until the mixture thickens. Remove from the heat.

Place the cane syrup in a small saucepan and heat to a simmer. Whisk about 2 tablespoons of the syrup into the custard, then whisk in the remaining syrup. Cool to room temperature, about 30 minutes. Stir in the cream and refrigerate for at least 1 hour or overnight.

Prepare as directed in a 1-quart ice cream maker, adding the pecans about halfway through churning. The ice cream will be soft, so place it in a resealable container and freeze until firm.

Easy Praline Ice Cream Topping

Sometimes you just need something simple and sweet. This will dress up a bowl of ice cream with very little effort.

MAKES 2 ½ CUPS

1 stick unsalted butter
1 cup packed light brown sugar
½ teaspoon salt
½ cup chopped pecans
2¼ cups cornflakes

Spread out a sheet of aluminum foil on a work surface.

Place the butter, brown sugar, and salt in a saucepan over medium heat. Heat, stirring, until the butter and sugar are melted and the mixture comes to a full bowl. Boil for 2 minutes.

Remove from the heat. Add the nuts and cornflakes and stir until the cornflakes are completely coated. Turn out onto the foil and spread into a thin layer. Let cool and break into chunks. Store in an airtight container, Serve sprinkled over vanilla or butter pecan ice cream. (It's fine at room temperature, but it's even better if you warm it for 30 seconds in a microwave.)

Orange-Cherry Pecan Bread

This makes a beautiful gift, with more flavor than most quick breads.

1 cup pecan halves, divided
1½ cups dried cherries
1 medium orange
⅔ cup buttermilk
6 tablespoons melted unsalted butter
1 large egg, lightly beaten
2 cups all-purpose flour
1 cup sugar
1 teaspoon salt
1 teaspoon baking powder
¼ teaspoon baking soda

Preheat the oven to 375°. Grease a 9-inch loaf pan.

Spread the pecans in a dry skillet over medium-low heat. Stir occasionally until toasted. (Watch carefully to make sure they don't burn.) Place ½ cup pecans and the dried cherries on a cutting board and chop coarsely.

Grate 1 tablespoon zest from the orange into a mixing bowl. (By grating directly into the mixing bowl, you get the essential oils from the orange, too.) Juice the orange and add ⅓ cup juice to the mixing bowl. Add the buttermilk, melted butter, and egg and stir together.

Whisk together the flour, sugar, salt, baking powder, and baking soda in a separate bowl. Add the orange juice mixture and stir with a rubber spatula just until moistened (some dry areas may remain). Gently stir in the chopped cherries and pecans. Spread the batter evenly in the prepared loaf pan. Chop the remaining ½ cup pecans coarsely and sprinkle over the batter.

Bake for 20 minutes. Reduce the heat to 350° and bake until golden and a toothpick inserted in the center comes out clean. Cool in the pan for 10 minutes, then remove from the pan and cool completely on a rack, about 1 hour.

Cinnamon-Pecan Coffee Cake with Strawberry-Pecan Butter

My friend Catherine Rabb once owned a Charlotte restaurant called Catherine's that was known for its brunch. This coffee cake was so popular, they had to make 2 dozen pans every day. I modified the strawberry butter, adding pecans and reducing the amount of butter. Don't skip the butter—it's positively decadent. (If you have leftover butter, try it on Townhouse crackers.)

MAKES 12 SERVINGS

FOR THE COFFEE CAKE
Nonstick cooking spray
2¼ cups all-purpose flour
½ teaspoon salt
2 teaspoons ground cinnamon
½ teaspoon ground ginger
1 cup packed light brown sugar
¾ cup granulated sugar
¾ cup vegetable or canola oil
1 cup coarsely chopped pecans
1 teaspoon baking powder
1 teaspoon baking soda
1 large egg
1 cup buttermilk

FOR THE STRAWBERRY-PECAN BUTTER
2 sticks unsalted butter, at room temperature
8 ounces strawberry preserves (not jam)
½–1 cup confectioners' sugar
½ cup coarsely chopped pecans

Preheat the oven to 350°. Spray a 13 × 9-inch baking pan with nonstick cooking spray.

Combine the flour, salt, cinnamon, ginger, brown sugar, and granulated sugar in a large mixing bowl. Add the oil and whisk until well mixed and a little crumbly. Place ¾ cup of the mixture in a smaller bowl and add the pecans.

Add the baking powder, baking soda, egg, and buttermilk to the remaining flour mixture in the large bowl. Stir together quickly, but don't overmix. (You may have a few lumps, which are fine.)

Spread the batter evenly in the prepared baking pan. Sprinkle the reserved pecan mixture evenly over the batter. Bake for about 40 minutes, until brown and the edges are coming away from the pan a little.

To make the Strawberry-Pecan Butter, beat the butter, strawberry preserves, and confectioners' sugar until the mixture looks like pink frosting. Stir in the chopped pecans. Keeps refrigerated for up to 1 week.

Serve warm or at room temperature with the butter.

Buttermilk-Pecan Waffles
with Pecan Syrup

Leftover waffles can be frozen and reheated easily in a toaster.

MAKES ABOUT 8 WAFFLES

1 cup coarsely chopped pecans, divided
1 cup maple syrup (preferably Grade B)
2 cups all-purpose flour
2 tablespoons sugar
1 teaspoon baking powder
½ teaspoon baking soda
½ teaspoon salt
2 large eggs
2 cups buttermilk
1 stick melted unsalted butter

Preheat the oven to 350° and place a wire rack over a baking sheet.

Place ¼ cup pecans and the maple syrup in a small saucepan. Keep warm over medium-low heat until ready to serve.

Whisk together the flour, sugar, baking powder, baking soda, and salt in a medium mixing bowl. Make a well in the center of the dry ingredients.

In a separate bowl, whisk together the eggs, buttermilk, and melted butter. Pour into the dry ingredients and stir briefly with a rubber spatula, just until combined; some lumps should remain. Stir in the remaining ¾ cup pecans.

Heat a waffle iron according to manufacturer's directions. Pour a generous ⅓ cup batter on the iron, close, and cook until the steam stops coming out of the sides and the waffle is brown. Remove from the grid and place on the wire rack over the baking sheet. Place in the oven to keep warm. Continue making the waffles with the remaining batter, adding the finished waffles to the rack in the oven to keep warm. Serve the waffles hot with the warm pecan syrup and butter.

Microwave Pecan Brittle

Baking soda gives this a lighter, crispier texture than boiled-sugar brittles. Make sure you have the pan prepared and waiting before you start because as soon as you add the soda, it needs to be spread quickly.

MAKES ABOUT 2 DOZEN PIECES

Nonstick cooking spray
$\frac{1}{2}$ cup light corn syrup
1 cup sugar
$1\frac{1}{2}$ cups pecan halves
1 teaspoon unsalted butter
1 teaspoon vanilla
$\frac{1}{4}$ teaspoon salt
1 teaspoon baking soda

Spray a rimmed baking sheet with nonstick cooking spray. (As long as you have the spray out, spray a 1 cup measuring cup, too—it makes it easier to get the corn syrup out.)

Combine the corn syrup and sugar in a 1½-quart round baking dish. Stir until blended. Microwave on high for 4 minutes. Remove from the oven and stir in the nuts. (Use oven mitts and handle the dish carefully. It will get hot as you continue to microwave the sugar mixture.)

Return to the microwave and cook for 4–6 minutes on high, until the sugar mixture is light brown. Stir in the butter, vanilla, and salt. Blend well. Microwave on high for 1–2 minutes.

Add the baking soda, sprinkling it quickly over the hot sugar. Stir gently just until foamy. Quickly pour out onto the prepared baking sheet. Let stand until completely cool. Break into pieces and store in an airtight container.

Acknowledgments

Many friends and colleagues turned out to have their own favorite pecan dishes and pecan lore. I offer my thanks to Catherine Rabb, Brenda Pinnell, Karen Garloch, Pam Kelley, Paula Wilkerson, Nancy McGinnis, Betty Lee, Rebecca Fant, Colleen Spencer, Peter St. Onge, and the entire *Charlotte Observer* newsroom for helping to eat all of those pecan dishes; John Williams and the Georgia Pecan Commission; Lenny Wells of the University of Georgia; and registered dietitians Carolyn O'Neil and Densie Webb.

I also have to thank my husband, Wayne Hill, and our son, Chris Hill, for eating pecans at breakfast, lunch, and dinner and never complaining or calling me "nuts."

Index